D0050937

Cows on the Farm

by Mari C. Schuh

Holstein cow

Consulting Editor: Gail Saunders-Smith, Ph.D.

Consultant: Donna Lange
Communication Programs Coordinator
Dairy Farmers of Ontario
Mississauga, Ontario

Pebble Books

an imprint of Capstone Press
Mankato, Minnesota

San Jose Public Library

Pebble Books are published by Capstone Press
151 Good Counsel Drive, P.O. Box 669, Mankato, Minnesota 56002
http://www.capstone-press.com

Copyright © 2002 Capstone Press. All rights reserved.
No part of this book may be reproduced without written permission
from the publisher. The publisher takes no responsibility for the use of any
of the materials or methods described in this book, nor for the products thereof.
Printed in the United States of America.

1 2 3 4 5 6 07 06 05 04 03 02

Library of Congress Cataloging-in-Publication Data
Schuh, Mari C., 1975–
    Cows on the farm / by Mari C. Schuh.
    p. cm.—(On the farm.)
    Includes bibliographical references (p. 23) and index.
    ISBN 0-7368-0992-9
    1. Cows—Juvenile literature. [1. Cows.] I. Title. II. Series.
SF197.5 .S38 2002
636.2—dc21   2001000467

Summary: Simple text and photographs present cows and how they are raised.

Note to Parents and Teachers

The series On the Farm supports national science standards related to life science. This book describes and illustrates cows on the farm. The photographs support early readers in understanding the text. The repetition of words and phrases helps early readers learn new words. This book also introduces early readers to subject-specific vocabulary words, which are defined in the Words to Know section. Early readers may need assistance to read some words and to use the Table of Contents, Words to Know, Read More, Internet Sites, and Index/Word List sections of the book.

Table of Contents

ears

udder

legs

hooves

4

Cows live on farms.

Jersey cow

Some farmers raise cows
for their meat.

Black Angus and Charolais cows

Some farmers raise cows
for their milk. Farmers
milk cows with machines.

Holstein cow

Veterinarians help
keep cows healthy.

Jersey cow and calf

Cows live in barns most of the winter.

Red Holstein cow

Farmers feed hay
and grain to cows.

Holstein cows

Cows graze in pastures.
They eat grass.

Holstein cows

Cows chew their cud.

Holstein cow

Cows moo.

Brown Swiss cow

Words to Know

barn—a building where animals, crops, and small pieces of equipment are kept

cud—food that has not been fully digested; cows bring up food from their stomach to chew again; then they swallow the food after it has been chewed again.

machine—a piece of equipment made of moving parts that is used to do a job

pasture—land that animals use to graze; to graze means to eat grass or other plants that are growing in a pasture or field.

raise—to care for animals as they grow and become older; some farmers raise cows for their meat; some farmers raise cows for their milk; people use cows' milk to make cheese and other products.

veterinarian—a doctor who treats sick or injured animals; veterinarians also check animals to make sure they are healthy.

Read More

Bell, Rachael. *Cows.* Farm Animals. Chicago: Heinemann Library, 2000.

Miller, Sara Swan. *Cows.* A True Book. New York: Children's Press, 2000.

Stone, Lynn M. *Cows Have Calves.* Animals and Their Young. Minneapolis: Compass Point Books, 2000.

Internet Sites

Agriculture for Kids
http://www.fsa.usda.gov/ca/agforkids.htm

Cow Printout
http://www.EnchantedLearning.com/subjects/mammals/farm/Cowprintout.shtml

Dairy Facts
http://www.mda.state.mi.us/kids/pictures/dairy

Index/Word List

barns, 13
chew, 19
cud, 19
eat, 17
farmers, 7, 9, 15
farms, 5
feed, 15
grain, 15
grass, 17
graze, 17
hay, 15
healthy, 11
help, 11
keep, 11
live, 5, 13
machines, 9
meat, 7
milk, 9
moo, 21
most, 13
pastures, 17
raise, 7, 9
some, 7, 9
veterinarians, 11
winter, 13

Word Count: 56
Early-Intervention Level: 8

Credits
Heather Kindseth, cover designer; Heidi Meyer, production designer;
    Kimberly Danger and Deirdre Barton, photo researchers

Capstone Press/Gary Sundermeyer, 6, 8
Craig Nelson/Pictor, 20
David F. Clobes, Stock Photography, 12, 14
PhotoDisc, Inc., cover
Photri-Microstock, 10
Unicorn Stock Photos/Andre Jenny, 16; Martin R. Jones, 18
Visuals Unlimited/Cheryl Jones, 1; Inga Spence, 4

Special thanks to Vicki Fleming and Adam and Jason Berndt, all of Elysian,
Minnesota, for their assistance with this book.